T0063908

IN MY OWN WORDS

MARLIN A. JONES

authorHOUSE®

AuthorHouse™ LLC
1663 Liberty Drive
Bloomington, IN 47403
www.authorhouse.com
Phone: 1-800-839-8640

Published by AuthorHouse 01/21/2014

ISBN: 978-1-4918-5339-9 (sc)
ISBN: 978-1-4918-5340-5 (e)

Library of Congress Control Number: 2014901125

TABLE OF CONTENTS

ACKNOWLEDGMENTS

I would like to thank Jesus Christ for allowing me to make mistakes, and in the midst of the storms you have still have shown me Favor, Grace, and Mercy. May You continue to guide my steps and place the right words within my Spirit. The Bible states that there is life and death in the tongue. In knowing that, may You be the source of my words and peace within my soul while I share my gift with the world. Thank You for life's lessons that have allowed me to grow, understand, and mature as a man. For His Love is the same Today, Tomorrow, and Forever . . . . Amen

I also want to thank those that have crossed my path over the years, despite the season, we've met at a crossroad; and we've all learned something along the way. Time is the only constant thing in the universe; change is the byproduct of us moving forward.

If it had not been for heartache, I would have not known how to love.
If it had not been for tears, I would have not known how to smile.
If it had not been for crying, I would not have known how to laugh.
If it had not been for pain, I would not have known peace.

If it had not been for those long sleepless nights, I would not have been able to reflect on my actions, and make the necessary changes.

We are here for a short time, so understand that life is about the living, it's about mistakes, and it's about growth and with growth . . . change. We are like the seasons, what once was, shall never be the same again.

I would like to thank those that have pulled me aside and given me words of encouragement; those that have corrected me when needed, and those that have allowed me to make mistakes and still had enough love for me to forgive me. It is those people that I will forever be indebted too; it is those people that will help change the world person by person and community by community. It's what the world desperately needs today.

A heartfelt thanks to Mike/Linda Mcnair, Anna Citino, and Debbie Wojnarski for believing in me, encouraging me, and directing me along the way while exploring my new endeavors of the fashion world—thank you for your time and unselfish acts of kindness you've shown me.

To my children, Marcus and Taylor Jones, you have made me a proud father, before you know it you two will be adults creating families of your own. I would like you too understand that mistakes are a part of life and they are designed to mold and make us better people. I Love you both!

To Helen Jones, words can never say thank you enough for what you have given our children, with that I say "Thank You."

And a very special thanks to my mother, Denise Robinson, for your undying love and support on all things that I have done and continue to do. For that I am grateful for your wisdom and encouraging me to do the right things despite my emotions. You are the strongest woman I know and for that I Love You!

In Memory of:
MARCUS A. JONES

May you rest in peace
13 April 1970 - 10 Sept. 1996

DEDICATION

Standing in the same place
For a long long time
If our hands go the wrong way
I hope your hearts still mine
Even when the sunsets
And the stars fade from view
What I've given was true
As the night falls
And the tears brand new
Know that our love was real and true.

This book defines a more personal journey than I have ever expressed in the past. So with that, I dedicate this book too those that still believe in love. May she wander along your path and follow you home, where she may dwell forever.

ABOUT THE BOOK

Marlin's creativity extends well beyond the fashion world and parallels his writings. I hope reading his poetry will help you to understand and appreciate his metaphorical vernacular. Marlin has found inspiration in writing not only poetry, but in general. One thing is true words are powerful . . . he hopes to reach, inspire, and provoke thought on his journey to find balance in life and love, as we navigate through the mountains and valleys of life.

Welcome to his world . . .

INTRODUCTION

"We struggle daily with matters of the heart trying to make sense of our feelings, and if I continue to do that, then love will be just a place I've visited.". . . . Marlin Jones

YOU

Your face captures the sunlight
And your eyes rival the stars
Your smile like the morning dew
As your kisses melt my heart
Your lips like the rain,
And your soul has depth like the sea
Your laugh penetrates my being
Your touch discovers me.
You are the meaning of love
The definition of life
Without you I don't exist
And without you love has no spark
To think I've existed all this time and to have never
experienced life
For you are the air that I breathe, the sound of reason in
my ear, and the wind
Beneath my wings during flight
Time stands still while I'm in your space

Like the stars in the sky just past the Milky Way

If it weren't for YOU not sure where I'd be

Perhaps lost in this world . . . . wandering aimlessly

You mean more to me than I could ever imagine

You complete me, make me whole and that's all that matters

You plus me and together we are one

Me without you, is like the world without the Son

My life complete and my dreams came true

Not by fate or by chance, but because of YOU

DOUBT

Why do we long for tomorrow

When we know not what tomorrow brings.

Why do we long to fall in love . . .

When we know not what we give will be returned.

We live with expectation, but never give enough to accept fate.

To trust, we must relinquish doubt.

But to love . . . . . . we must give of ourselves completely.

THE TRUTH

Words are nothing without feelings
Feelings are nothing without touch
Smiles are nothing without thoughts
The sun is nothing without the sky
Night does not exist without the day
The moon is nothing without the stars
Life is nothing without death
Laughter is nothing without crying
Love is nothing without you

QUESTIONS . . .

I want to know if you can love beyond your imagination or do you imagine being in love.

I want to know if you can cry for someone else, even though the pain isn't yours . . .

I want to know if your dreams are in black and white . . . for life is in living color.

I want to know if your days are lonely or do you long for days past.

I want to know if you day dream or dream of days to come . . .

I want to know if you long to be in someone's arms or if you keep someone at arm's length.

I want to know does your heart beat for love or is it beating just to live . . .

I want to know your fears or do you fear what someone knows.

I want to know can you love without regret or do you regret not loving . . .

I want to know if love with every ounce of your being or do you give your heart in pieces.

I want to know if my voice is music to your soul or do you need music to discover that from within . . .

I want to know if your arms are lonely when I'm in them or are they lonely when I'm not.

I want to know if your smile is for me or do you smile when I'm not around . . .

I want to know have you ever experienced true love or is true love not your experience.

I want to know if you love me or do you love the idea of me loving you.

These are the questions I want to know or do you question what you want to tell me . . .

I want to know do you love unconditionally or does your love have conditions . . .

I want to know the truth or is there no truth in you, for you have evaded detection and captured my heart; may the words you feel introduce themselves in the physical.

These are just a few questions I want to know . . .

WORDS

My desires ignore my patience

For my words are more than phrases

They are frequencies of energy manifested in speech

Created in places not seen by light

But created from the morning sun

As I journey in space not consumed by time, but relative to
the physical

As our bodies bond . . . not by that which is tangible, but
by that which is connected

As we share our thoughts

Our words become one

REASONS . . .

Time drifts like water, as the day ushers in the night.
Forced to leave in order to grow . . . as my heart is forced to fight.
For every day I awake and your not close, is every breathe I take as I begin to choke.
Truth has left . . . as regret stands near
Saturated by pain . . .
My arms raised in fear.
Sunshine expected as the clouds roll bye
Void replaced by contentment . . . formulated in my mind.
Weathered by the storm, conditioned by time
My soul can bear no more as I am introduced to my pride.
Alone has paid me a visit, more than I care to know
We are like seeds in barren soil . . . often forced to grow.
Nurtured by the elements, consumed by the clock . . .
As the season pass, it is shorter than we thought.
As you deserve better than what I was able to give,
As you forgive my actions . . . . . . my words stand still.

MY THOUGHTS

Torn and hard to leave

My heart wants to stay

My dreams are the doorway

Footprints lost in the snow

Suspended in thought

Forgotten memories revisited . . .

Chasing what defines us, but leaving what has made us

Your love has kept me safe from the world.

Your hands have guided me through the storm.

Your words have provided me strength.

Your touch affirms I'm alive.

Home is where you are.

I cry not because I'm sad.

I cry because I am free.

Places I've gone, streets I've wandered, valley's I've kneeled
and mountains I've climbed

Here I am today . . .

Changed by my thoughts.

CONNECTED

Given without question
Trusted without doubt
Loved without reason
Forgiven without thought
What I am you are
What I give you've gotten
What I want You have
What I know you've known
To love is to be loved
Your smile captures me
Your kiss discovers me
Your touch defines me
Your love inspires me
What we know physically we share spiritually

LOVE DEFINED

Manifested thru touch

Invoked by emotion

The unknown of each other

Are new places to discover . . .

The wind tells stories

While the rain reminds us

The sun assures our existence

While the night peaks our interest

Death is the reason why we live

As the night falls like tears

As our spirituality transcends the Heavens

Because of you . . .

Love is defined

NO INTRODUCTION NEEDED

We live in 3 worlds

The eyes

The mind

And the heart

In constant battle, we struggle to maintain.

As the physical realm somehow jades my senses

For reason not clear, to my thoughts

For reality has connection to my dreams

As my emotions speak

No introduction needed . . .

Love has arrived.

IMAGINE

We are bound by our thoughts
Lifted thru imagination
Our dreams take us place that the mind can't understand
Its reach extends beyond the clouds
Acting as a ladder connecting two worlds
Places not seen by human hands but within arm's reach
A place where time and space don't exist
We are transformed

THAT PLACE

Feelings without love is an empty place
Smiles without connection is an empty space
The sky with no moon is no site at all
Life without death is not living at all
Laughter without crying is not laughing at all
Love without you, is like a season without fall
To love is an action, but to receive love is a gift
That place I speak of, is where dreams are connected
And where love exists

IN BETWEEN WORDS

Your actions say things that your lips don't
Your arms tell me things that your heart won't
Your eyes take me places your feet can't
Your mind reveals secrets that your hugs don't
Your touch tells me things that your kisses should
Your silence tells me things that are understood
We say things that words can't begin to explain
Like the wind changing direction past a weathervane
The less we say then the more we learn
The harder we fall the more we yearn
Words . . . .
Not the only thing we use to create life
But the closes thing to love that makes it alright.

LOVE SONG

If my words could talk

You would understand my pain

If my tears were music

Then you could hear my heart sing

If my touch revealed things about me that you didn't
even know

Even if my mouth was closed

My smile would still show

If my actions justified my words

Then the pain I caused, would be of very few words

If I'm sorry could explain itself

Then "I love you" would be more than enough

If I left this world tomorrow and didn't say goodbye

Then the stars would be my reason for looking up in
the sky

If I could love anyone . . . more than I did you

Then my heart would be whole and not held together
by glue

If I could start over from the first day we met

Then I wouldn't have to live with so much regret

ALIVE

We are like glass in solid form
And fragile in every way
We are like the moon at night
As it passes thru its phase
We are like the clouds in the sky
As the wind directs their path
We are like water in a puddle
As the rain collects in mass
We are like the tears of an eye
As a levy swells until it runs
We are like the shadows on a clear day . . . as directed by
the sun
We are echoes of sound
As it travels thru the air
We are like the trees as they sway
Back and forth as they play
We are only here for a short time
Like the seasons . . . as they come and go

We are on a path and sometimes hit a crossroad . . . As we discover who we are

We are a reflection of where we've been, but not defined as such.

We are forever striving to be better

I don't think that's asking too much

We are what we choose and no one determines that

We are from the earth that which we are made of

I'm sorry but that's a fact

We are our words and our actions

So be careful what you give

We are the laughs and our smiles

A far better way to have lived

We are what we are

As my hands come together in thought

My head bowed, my eyes closed

And my prayers said out loud.

As I pray to the most high for Salvation and His grace

As I ask for protection while standing in this space.

BROKEN HEARTS . . .

Built upon words
Destroyed by the same
Turmoil leads to confusion
As insanity turns into pain
Lost in a familiar place
Reflection confirms my name
As my eyes react with fear
My tears turned into rain
My heart speaks louder
Drowned out by the same
Forgotten photos revisited
Love letters offset the pain
You are the reason I smile
The reason I live
The reason that God has blessed me with this gift
To share with the world, but more importantly you
How you have changed my life, by just being you.

CROSSROADS

Transformed by struggle
Conviction brings truth
Conformed by my thoughts
My reality is proof
Dreams connected
My fears produced
My steps are chosen
But my options are few
No chance to look back
My eyes won't view
My past behind me
Not sure about you
Which road I choose
Will be determined by fate
Which race I run
Will be won upon Grace
As Favor is given
Mercy falls into place
We are blessed beyond words
But cursed just the same

DREAMS . . .

Illusive as the shadows

But more compelling than anything else

Mysterious as the clouds, her touch felt unlike anything else

For her arrival is not by chance, but connection to my space

Caught off guard by her persistence, as my thoughts wander off in space

May she introduce herself to me

Or continue to be my mistress every night

No name given, as my eyes open and I finally see the light

When I awake her presence felt no more and no kiss left to say goodbye

As she courts me in my sleep, is where she meets me every night

May today we connect for once and for all

For my heart knows her name and she's the one I call

For destiny has found me, in this so called realm of time
Favored by the stars for her destiny has finally met mine
No introduction needed for we are familiar to each other
Her hand in mine as they complement one another
Truly she is felt . . . as my mind leaves the physical world
too connect
May I never return but live in her world forever
I'm sorry to be so direct
But I've longed for you more than you will ever know
As our dreams are our meeting place
And my pillow is the door.

SET FREE

Our eyes speak a language . . .

That the ears wouldn't understand.

Our hearts are the receiver . . . as the mind can't comprehend

My tears escape their prison under locked down for far too long

My emotions stir like a storm . . .

Never knew this would day would come.

My soul in denial held captive by my thoughts.

My life turned upside down as my fears run about . . .

What has brought me this far will never BE denied

As the tears make puddles on my pillow as I sleep . . . as I was drowning inside.

Released from the grips of what has been my life . . .

Set free by the grace of God for I have finally seen the light.

Forgiven is the measure

As I rebuild and let go

For love is what I've received as my smile begins to show

Forgiveness is the place that I hope to end up

As I check my ego and my pride at the door and evict them from my gut

No scarlet letter will ever be displayed

No matter the struggle for my foundation has already been laid

Paved for us all that will seek the truth

For it was because of HIM that I live and will make HIM my root

Growth within me has been allowed to live and overcome

My today is tomorrow as my yesterday has already begun

For now I'll move forward to never look back

For life is about the journey, despite the places we've visited

But ultimately where we end up . . .

BREATHE

Its properties are needed . . .

To ensure we are alive.

One thing I can't live without . . .

Next to looking in your eyes

Necessary to live . . .

But will certainly die if not.

No one knows its importance . . .

Seem as though we forgot.

What makes us laugh and sometimes even cry.

That something so transparent is necessary to survive

Like friction over a surface or resistance noted in flight

Like the wings of a bird soaring high above the mountain top

The concept is very clear no confusion around

For without it life hangs in the balance

And that theory is profound.

As I ponder my thoughts . . .

And collect my fears,

Without you there's no me . . . . that's all I'm saying here.

Important to life just as you are to me

As I open my mouth and inhale . . . is when I start to breathe.

THROUGH THE STORM

You are where Angels dwell . . .

Where human hands can't reach, but where prayers are abundant

You are where the Son sits . . .

May you watch over me, for my tears are only what eyes can see

May your hand comfort my broken body, for my heart has lost it's rhythm

You left without notice and I didn't get a chance to say goodbye . . .

May you save a place for me, for everything I am was taken with you.

May God have Mercy on my soul, for all I want is to be by your side

May this day never be forgotten, as tomorrow my life begins.

CHANGE

My eyes closed

My mind makes a wish

Held captive by your smile

Consumed by my thoughts

Truth brings peace

Hope allows me to feel

The light defines your touch

As my heart speaks . . .

My soul responds

Life's journey has brought me to my knees

Change has allowed me to stand .

I WILL FOLLOW

The sun has come and the rain has left
The day brand new, as the weary slept
You are my light . . .
My way,
No other path shall I follow . . .
My hope restored and every breathe I take
That lump in my throat when I swallow
My dreams . . .
My sunset
My rainbow in the sky
The sound of laughter within my soul
My rock . . . my foundation as my dreams unfold
Today approaching . . . . tomorrow so close
Forever introduced as the night draws close

END OF THE ROAD

Conviction felt in every word

As my pen begins to weep

My words find refuge on the page

As my heart begins to speak

What was taken was given . . . . no crime to report

The lighthouse signals as the ship veers close, deterring its approach

Emotions written

Reflections of pain

Effortlessly words flow, despite the coming of the rain

When I awoke and found you gone

Now I know the difference between a house and home

Wish we could back to a time when we first met

When we used to forgive and forget

Sorry I never showed you, assumed you'd always be there

So hard to let go

And now we've come to the end of the road

DEAR HEAVENLY FATHER,

I come to you with a sad heart and many prayers for this world. We are a world of senseless violence, greed and disparity. We have turned our backs on YOU for selfish reasons; and then ask how a loving and compassionate God would allow such terrible things to happen in this world to innocent men, women, and children; as we escort You out of our schools, homes, and public events for the sake of not offending others. Then choose to blame you for the world events. There are people in this world that would rather worship material things, money and ideologies then to believe that YOU are The Only Begotten Son sent to Earth to die for the sins of the world. Father you are the Creator of life, The Prince of Peace, The Most High, Lord of Lords and Kings of Kings. May Your Mercy and Grace endure forever.

I ask you to "Forgive them for they know not what they do" and ask that you to heal our land, homes, schools and our hearts. The Bible states that wherever two or more agree is where you will dwell. I stand here in the gaps for the voiceless, for the sick, those not of sound mind, and the corrupt at heart.

I ask you Father that you bless and keep our families safe and hide us from the enemy. I ask for your Favor, Mercy, and Grace. I ask that you heal our nation and its people for we are a nation hurting. I ask that we humble ourselves before You and reject the name of pride, but kneel before the throne of God and repent our sins. For there will come a day when we will stand before YOU, and may you have Mercy on our souls. For You are The Way, Truth and The Light and that NO ONE cometh to the Father except thru YOU, Jesus Christ, The One and only Begotten Son.

All those who agree . . . . .

Say,

Amen

MARLIN A. JONES

The
Definition of A Man
Tribulations of the heart

This book is a thought-provoking, honest, and heartfelt poetry in narrative form, that will captivate the reader into something that we are all familiar with... love, heartbreak, and growing into one's self. Inspired by years of putting my thoughts on paper, I am now ready to share this most sacred part of myself with the world, as a way to inspire and help with healing and moving forward.

Notes

Notes